Through
the
Fields

A journey through life
seasoned with prayer

by

LAURA R. HESS

To John,
celebrate your life
Tell your story
Peace, joy, love
in Christ
Laura R. Hess
June 1998

"wingborne"
diaconal productions
York, Pennsylvania

1996

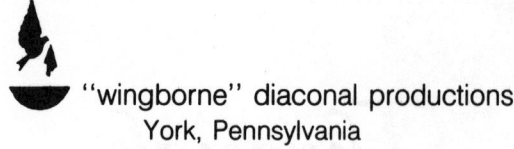

"wingborne" diaconal productions
York, Pennsylvania

*is a small publisher dedicated to providing items
that contribute to individual growth and spirit...*

Other publications:

"Call My Name . . . Take My Hand"
Recipes for Caregivers
1st printing © 1991
2nd printing 1994

Linking Links: Persons Who Prepare Others for Caregiving
Plans for Teaching Children, Teens, and Adults
Copyright © 1992

*The Linker, Directions for the
Director of Family Events*
"Link the Generations with Love"
Copyright © 1993

"Wingborne" Trilogy — Off the Page Into Action
Copyright © 1994

Through
the
Fields

*A journey through life
seasoned with prayer*

"MY GOD AND I"

My God and I go through the fields together
We walk and talk as good friends should and do
We clasp our hands, our voices ring with laughter
My God and I walk through the meadow's hue;
We clasp our hands, our voices ring with laughter
My God and I walk through the meadow's hue.

He tells me of the years that went before me,
When heavenly plans were made for me to be,
When all was but a dream of dim conception
To come to life, earth's verdant glory see;
When all was but a dream of dim conception
To come to life, earth's verdant glory see.

My God and I will go for aye together,
We'll walk and talk and jest as good friends do;
This earth will pass, and with it common trifles
But God and I will go unendingly;
This earth will pass, and with it common trifles
But God and I will go unendingly.

—Austris A. Wihtol

DEDICATION

Dedicated to Christian Educators
who met in San Antonio

October 1996

to

"Remember the PAST
to craft the FUTURE
so as to transform the PRESENT
and go forth
SINGING GOD'S SONG IN A NEW LAND"

and

To each who nurture children,
eager teens and young adults
and care for aging parents.

TABLE OF CONTENTS

PROLOGUE

PROLOGUE

Life begins for us all with God who is the God of every child born of love "For beloved, God is Love." We are intended by God to journey through many growing stages: birth, childhood, adolescence, adult - young, middle, old. The pilgrim journey unfolds with no promise of uniformity - for we are as different/unique as each of every age and station. If we are lucky, we naturally or with help achieve each task from cradle to grave.

Each has a vocational journey. Mine, Christian Education. At every turn in the road, it necessitates careful, prayerful listening to assess where God is leading.

It is my hope that my journey may call you, the reader, to many recollections of your peaks and valleys - bringing at times a smile, a tear, a time to tell YOUR STORY!

WHY I AM REALLY WRITING THIS BOOK

You may remember the hymn written by Charles Wesley that asks "AND ARE WE YET ALIVE?" As one comes to the close of a long career, to find that life holds at least another twenty years, one cannot become irrelevant, diminished, infirm! I am yet alive and hope for entry into the 21st Century, bringing from the past that which may in some small way affect the future.

I believe as I have since the beginning of my career in the church as Director of Youth Work for Central Pennsylvania Conference, that "EACH NEW GENERATION IS ANOTHER GOD-GIVEN OPPORTUNITY TO LIFT MANKIND TOWARD GOD."

My generation has seen great strides. We are nearer the reality of the world, a global village; the Cold War over; the

Berlin Wall down. I would like to say strides in race relations, but sadly there are "miles to go, before we sleep."

I have confidence that this generation stepping up to bat will be unafraid of change, and will do great things to turn about the troubles of Society - AIDS, drugs, crime, prejudicial *isms*, homelessness - that affect us all.

If I can in any way help them FIND THEIR WAY, HAVE A CAUSE, SET THEIR DIRECTION FIRMLY WITH FAITH, I shall be content.

And how do those of each new generation find God's purpose and direction from basic commitment to serve Him? Follow.

Abraham went out not knowing whither he went. Jacob wrestled with the angel!

Seeking to find in God's HISTORY BOOK an eventual reality, that HIS STORY can become OUR STORY, leads me to RECLAIM MY JOURNEY from a stack of Journals, kept intermittently through the years - no different from any who dares to "go out, not knowing whither they would go."

TRACKING A PROFESSION

When Christian Education Fellowship was in its infant days, it resided in the midst of a larger body that met as the Conference on Christian Education Novembers and in Grand Rapids, MI. Gathered here were Annual Conference Staff from across the Church who had responsibility for Children, Youth, Camping, Adult ministries, Executive Secretaries, and College and Seminary professors. Each of these met separately within the larger Conference. At that time the "baby" of Christian Education, local church Directors of Christian Education numbering some 30 persons, went forth on the journey that brings us where we are today. Southeastern Jurisdiction led the way. Many large Sunday Schools numbering into the thousands needed professional staff, and were in part supported by the World Service dollar relegating near half to Education. This was not a new profession in major urban areas across the country, e.g. Riverside Church, NYC, First Methodist Church, Evanston, IL.

There are a few among us from that day -- Jane Batts, Nina Reeves, from the Methodist tradition and others who have a story to tell from the Evangelical United Brethren tradition. These will attest, with stories and dreams, how the Christian Education profession made its sure effective assent in the heart of Churches and Conference and Jurisdictions across the Nation - a journey of 50 years. Peaks and valleys mark the half century trek, early undergirded by the visionary, Walter Towner and soon to be daring leader of CEF, R. Harold Hipps, developer of Gatherings designed to be on the cutting edge of the Church's ministry, following the highest Christian Call and Challange each era presented.

How did one get from a Christian Educator in Central Pennsylvania to the Christian Education Conference in Grand Rapids, 1948 to San Antonio, 1996?

From a first local church Christian Education position in Florida Conference, and throughout a career in Christian Education, SELDOM WERE CHRISTIAN EDUCATORS LEFT WITHOUT A SUPPORTIVE, AFFIRMING FELLOWSHIP ACROSS THIS HALF-CENTURY AND AS WE PREPARE FOR 2001!

THROUGH THE FIELDS contains very personal glimpses into the journey of another seeker of The Way. If you find that your path crosses mine, may you have a clearer view over the valley, hillside, mountain-top and beyond. Your journey, too, is marked with emotion, reason, truth. God goes before. You can find The Way.

Let these pages fall open wherever. Make your notes, collect your photos and illustrations. Pass them on to those who follow after you - a legacy unlike any other anywhere, because it is from YOU!

The Child's Appeal

I am the Child,
You hold in your hand my destiny.
You determine, largely, whether I shall succeed or fail.
Give me, I pray you, those things that make for happiness.
Train me, I beg you, that I may be a blessing to the world.

—Mamie Gene Cole

Chapter 1
"NOW I LAY ME . . ."

It is debatable how sure or vivid memories of early childhood are. Some suggest that stories are told by fond family members of your early adventures - first word, first step. I can't believe I remember sitting on my Grandfather's lap, on the porch swing, reaching for the gold chain of his pocket watch. They say he held it to my ear so I could hear its steady tic-toc-tic-toc! He died soon after. It was the first visit to my paternal grandparents' house! But not the last. My visits assured me the center of attention. The "cute" antics, relayed to neighbors and friends, were later confirmed when a newspaper clipping was produced, yellow with age. A real nugget - When I was kitchen-table high, I was cautioned lest I bump my *cranium* on the table. Language development called for my response: *"You mean my BEAN?"* I would rather be cuddled and hugged at that age! None the less, the impressions made caused me early to find my way across two streets and visit on my own! Grandmother always had ten o'clock coffee and white toast. Nought could arouse my mother's alarm more, and upon returning home yardsticks were administered. Was I learning right from wrong!

I cannot remember when, but I was taught to pray. Maybe I even kneeled to say:

> *"Now I lay me down to sleep.*
> *I pray the Lord my soul to keep.*
> *If I should die before I wake*
> *I pray the Lord my soul to take."*

I presume adding to it ". . . *And God bless mama and daddy and grandma and grandpa.* AMEN."

I could have wondered: What is soul? Why die in my sleep? I'm not sure a child would find at bed-time a loving caring

God! Maybe he was so loving that he would truly want me. Most important at that early age was the rhythm and sounds - not the depth of "meanings." Yet for me it meant God might punish me for running away from home. Much more goes on in a little head that learns to talk with God.

Lovely is the children's hymn:

FATHER WE THANK THEE

Father, we thank Thee for the night,
And for the pleasant morning light,
For rest and food, and loving care,
And all that makes the day so fair.

Help us to do the things we should
To be to others kind and good;
In all our work and all our play,
To love Thee better every day.

From 1894 book of SONGS AND STUDY FOR GOD'S LITTLE ONES. *Henry B. Noyes & Co., Boston.*

Chapter 2
WE CAN'T LEAVE NOW: IT'S MY TURN TO PRAY!

It was a memorable time - Depression Years, but what would a ten-year-old know? Poor? Not us! We ate well. Meat on Sunday and maybe on Wednesday. Milk and butter, and brown bread, plenty of vegetables sustained us. Health-conscious parents - dietitian and drugless therapist - DESTINED US HEALTHY!

Other occurrences changed the course of our family life. Dad's income dwindled. We rented out my room. My sister and I had to share! Family decisions would separate us! Mother would go to work 100 miles away. Dad would care for my sister and me. When school was out, we would join mother in the Poconos!

Summer at Camp Paupac! We were together again in one big room in the Lodge of the Girls Camp. Dad was camp doctor. Mother commuted to work. Swimming, canoeing, baiting the line with worms to catch fish! Flash flood! Tents blown down! September 1, address Chestnut Burr Cottage, off Main St., Mt. Pocono. Across the street our school, three grades in each! Up the street Church and Sunday School. Winter time ice-skating on Bisbing's Pond, collecting Bing Crosby pictures, listening to Captain Tim Healy Stamp Collector, and Amos 'n Andy on radio! Shopping in Stroudsburg once a month!

Every day was rife with new experiences. Mother seriously ill with pneumonia. Nurse came. We children were sent to stay with folks down the hill, till crisis was passed. Sub-zero temperatures. Death of a little girl. Why? Crush on the boy up the street! Onset of puberty! Changing body! Expanding world!

Winter turned to Spring. Wildflowers bloomed in our woods - lady slippers, trillium, skunk cabbage! School ended. Preparations were being made to return to our home. There might be time to attend Vacation Bible School. I would be in 6th grade class. We had to do three things: Learn the Books of the Bible; embroider the map of Israel, and learn to pray! Each morning ended with a student praying aloud. Could I? At night I would practice in the stillness of my bedroom. Unaware that time was drawing near to visit grandparents and our old home, I was distraught, for this was the day I WOULD PRAY ALOUD! "WE CAN'T LEAVE NOW! IT'S MY TURN TO PRAY!!"

Pre-adolescence is an awesome time! What must it be like for the chrysalis to break and the butterfly struggle, wet and alone in a new environment, not really knowing it was born to fly!

Learned the Quaker saying from a plaque hanging in our room in Camp Paupac Lodge, Tobyhanna, PA.

"EVERYONE'S QUEER BUT ME AND THEE
AND SOMETIMES I THINK THEE IS TOO!"

WHAT IS PRAYER?

Prayer is the soul's sincere desire,
Uttered or unexpressed;
The motions of a hidden fire,
That trembles in the breast.

Prayer is the burden of a sigh
the falling of a tear;
The upward glancing of an eye,
When none but God is near.

Prayer is the simplest form of speech
That infant lips can try;
Prayer, the sublimest strains that reach
The Majesty on high.

O, Thou by whom we come to God -
The Life, the Truth, the Way!
The path of prayer Thyself hast trod;
Lord, teach us how to pray!

Definition of prayer by Scottish poet James Montgomery (1771-1854): a definition parents and grandparents may well have commited to memory!

Chapter 3
DAD'S PRAYERS

A question I ask from time to time, and in many different settings: *"What was your family table like when you were growing up?"* It is a good conversation starter, frequently met with instant response, revealing an array of family systems.

Weekdays we ate in the kitchen. Sundays in the dining room. Dad sat at the head of the table and said Grace as we bowed our heads. I remember his *"Bless this food to its intended use and save us through Christ, AMEN..."* We were allowed to invite friends to eat with us. They would bow their heads dutifully, then end by crossing themselves. Occasionally they would be invited to pray: *Bless us, O Lord and these Thy Gifts, which we are about to receive from thy Bounty. Through Christ our Lord.*

Dad was respected by neighbor families. It was he who built our house and one for mother's parents next door. Each Christmas Eve he would play Santa Claus all over the neighborhood. I don't recall how old I was when I discovered Santa's hands were just like my father's! Across the years when visiting back home at Christmas, neighbors would recall with delight the childhood visits with Santa Claus!

Parents are special people. A family is unique. Children are a challenge! Mountains and valleys; heights and depths are inevitable. Love, the glue that holds it all together through crises of unbelievable proportions, needs constant nourishment. Dad and Mother shared devotions with each other. I don't remember ever being a part of family prayer. It was the era when children should be seen and not heard, and did not participate in adult activities. Dad taught Lutheran Sunday School, Mother grew up Methodist with six brothers and sisters. There were many family extremities, but a memorable one came when I was thirteen. An unidentifiable eye problem refused to respond to any known treatment. My parents' prayer was taught to me, and Dad would nightly pray with me while Mother tucked my sister in bed.

Many times I shared this prayer with others, but not until recently did I find an ally - Bishop Felton May, ready to go to Washington to fight drug problems in that city, shared this Prayer with us at the time of his departure. It was his farewell message from the pulpit of Camp Curtin/Mitchell Memorial Church in Harrisburg!

THE PRAYER OF FAITH

God is my help in every need
God does my every hunger feed
God walks beside me - guides my way
Through every moment of the day.
I now am wise - I now am true,
Patient, kind, and loving, too.
All things I am can do and be
Through Christ the Truth which is in me.
God is my health. I can't be sick
God is my strength, unfailing, quick.
God is my all. I know no fear
Since God and Love and Truth are here.

SCRAPBOOK GLEANINGS

From the pen of Margaret Sanger

I have an altar, a curious shrine
    Unlike any other I've known,
On its surface no chill waxen lilies have bloomed,
    no tall pallid candles have shone.
It is cheery with friendship's
    warm, amber and rose,
And I know the glow never will fade
  For there's nothing that lasts
    Like the smile and the clasp
  Of the hand of which friendship is made.

It is my joy in life to find
    At every turning of the road,
The strong arm of a comrade kind,
    To help me onward with my load.
And since I have no gold to give,
    And love alone must make amends,
My only prayer is, while I live
  GOD MAKE ME WORTHY OF MY FRIENDS!

The Labyrinth–
Is There a Map?

Never has adolescence been an easy way. Reader, looking back, how was it for you? The field was often rocky, filled with pit-falls, and walking through unsteady. Yet special gifts along the way served to shape the days when new-found YOU came into existence...Each of us name events that become a milestone from which we move into a serious time of plying our skills, growing with new responsibilities.

Chapter 4
DIRE STRAITS

What happens when an eager 7th grader - before her second month of school - comes down with a rare eye disease, corneal ulcers? What is it like to cringe in sunlight, travel from specialist to specialist for help and healing, hearing that after a six-month ordeal surgery might be the only answer, not precluding eventual blindness?

Food and vitamins were gorged. Many prayed. Visitors brought Sunday School papers, and a large print collection of PSALMS, which I memorized. School must have gone wanting for I have no recollection of one text-book. Best medicine during the room-bound, darkened day, was administered when 4:00 came. Catholic School was out, and faithful friend, Cynthia, a year younger, would come. We talked and laughed, played Bible memory games, cut up magazines, made scrap-books, memorized poems, told stories, and planned seasonal programs to do for the crippled man down the street!

No one could have known my goal: to read the New Testament through. Catholics were not allowed to own a Bible at that time. It was a privilege to have one! Over the months I achieved my goal - to the end of Revelation! Squinting in dim light, before going to sleep.

Nor could any one have known my prayer:

"GOD, I WILL DO ANYTHING FOR YOU IF I CAN ONLY HAVE MY SIGHT!"

Prayers began to be answered. In April a new vitamin was found. Healing began. Sweet relief from itchy eyes. In two weeks back to school, with only scars left, impairing vision minusculely! They would fade.

Quiet determination to follow a commitment to God would begin!

Dare one bargain with God?? Jacob did, and walked away from angel-wrestling, with only a limp!

FROM MY SCRAPBOOK:

Beneath a picture of Hoffman's head of Christ is the following:

JESUS THE HELPER

He is ready to aid when we pray,
He will do what we ask him to do;
When we show him our plan, when we tell him our task
He will help, if our hearts are true,
For his love is deep, and his arm is strong,
And his hand will guide us, our whole life long.

—Nancy Byrd Turner

Somebody CARES!
What a world of woe
Lifts from our hearts
When we really know
That somebody cares
That we're in another's
Heart and prayers
I want you to know -
And you really do -
That somebody always
Is CARING FOR YOU!!

FROM MY JOURNAL:

Affliction best communicates the love of God. Jesus said, upon healing the blind man: "He's blind for this moment that my Father's works might be made manifest. Many are the afflictions of the righteous. In their affliction, they seek Me early."

JULY 9, 1960

I KNOW NOT WHAT EACH NEW EXPERIENCE MEANS
NOR DO I SEE THE END IN GAIN OR GLORY
BUT THIS I KNOW: WITH FAITH BELIEVING
THOU ART GOD WHO WORKS IN WONDROUS WAYS
TO OPEN THE WELLSPRING OF LIFE
TO ALL THY CHIDREN, WHEN THEY WRESTLE,
SEEK, AND FIND THEE, SEEKING THEM!

Chapter 5
FLOWERS GATHERED – THE HIGHER TENDERNESS

High school years for me held exciting experiences. At church it was Queen Esthers, Standard Bearers, MYF. Always on the phone. Always busy going and coming. Carrie Barge House Party, writing Crowning of the Queen Ceremony, being selected to represent Central Pennsylvania at National Conference of Methodist Youth in Warrington, Mo. First train trip!! Frank Littell was president. Met Dorothy Jean Furnish, later to become professor of Christian Education, Garrett Seminary. Herman Will, World Peace Leader. We were in midst of war. Berlin had been bombed. We were *against Conscription!* I was cautioned about radical ideas. Radical, maybe, but the women need not have worried. I was keeping notes and ingesting things like:

The formula, ICOO. It stands for – IN CONSIDERATION OF OTHERS. A Missions School teacher, Hannah P. Miller, first put it on "my" chalk board!

And something special about old Jacob, who directed his sons, on a trip to Egypt for grain, to take to Pharaoh "A LITTLE BIT OF HONEY, AND BALM AND SPICE." That special instructor called these LIFE'S OVERTONES!

Remember! Practice them!

Friendships were of utmost importance, and grew deeper and dearer, eliciting prayers such as the following:

PRAYER PERFECT

Dear Lord, kind Lord, gracious Lord, I pray
Thou wilt look on all I love, tenderly today!
Weed their hearts of weariness; scatter every care
Down a wake of angel-wings
Winnowing the air.

Bring unto the sorrowing all release from pain;
Let the lips of laughter overflow again:
And with all the needy O divide, I pray,
This vast measure of content that is mine today!

—James Whitcomb Riley, 1849-1916

My search for next steps - College? YES! But how? Where? My soul sister Cynthia, too, was pondering her days ahead. A poem: THE HIGHER TENDERNESS would keep us in touch across many years, for she would leave for the Convent, and I to Mansfield to become a teacher.

GOD BLESS YOU - words are empty things
We speak, and think not of our saying -
Yet in this phrase forever rings
The higher tenderness of praying.
It means so much - it means that I
Would have no CARE distress you
Nor have your heart tuned to a sigh
GOD BLESS YOU!

Chapter 6
LIGHTS OUT - PRAYER TIME!

I took out some old photos the other day. These were the counselors I had recruited when I was Director of Youth Work for our Central PA Conference. I had responsibility for summer youth events. (I forgot to say I taught home economics long enough to get a permanent teaching certificate, then answered God's call to serve in his Church!) The Board of Education allowed me winter reprieves from the ice-packed roads in Pennsylvania to begin work on my Master's Degree at Scarritt College.

THE UPPER ROOM, housed then in a lovely old mansion on 18th Ave., afforded me use of dictating equipment. While through the week Charles Layman was opening new vistas of the Bible, and Dr. Waltzer took his students on running leaps through Church History, I spent Saturdays writing letters to prospective camp counselors, and planning training meetings, and mailing discs to the office secretary in Harrisburg.

Church Camping draws to it capable, dedicated staff and thousands of young people in any given season. Many leaders made their commitment to "full-time Christian Service."

I shall not forget my first summer counseling experience in a Senior High Camp. I tried to look older than I really was to gain respect of some who were even older than I. It was Cabin Prayer Time on the first evening. One camper read John 14. We sang *"Nearer My God to Thee."* Whimpers from the bunk above me broke into sobs. Mary had lost her mother to death within the past year, and this was the hymn sung at her funeral! We tumbled from our bunks, clasped Mary's hand and each others'. We prayed aloud and in our hearts that God would comfort Mary. Tears abated. *Blest Be the Tie That Binds our hearts in Christian love.* Prayer time over. To sleep. We grew larger in God's love that night - a cabin of senior high girls.

Sung as campers descended from Vesper Hill at sunset time:

"FOLLOW THE GLEAM"

To the knights in the days of old
Keeping watch on the mountain height
Came a vision of the Holy Grail
And a voice through the waiting night
    Follow, Follow, Follow the Gleam
    Banners unfurled,
    O'er all the World
    Follow, Follow, Follow the Gleam
Of the Light that shall bring the dawn.

....Not until Bill Waltzer's Church History Class in Grad School did I learn the origin of that song, sacred to many who answered that call! - to follow Christ into ministry mission and education or simply in the daily walk.

Testing Waters- Trying Wings

World War II and aftermath would affect those of my generation unwittingly. At best, we needed to meet each daily crisis not from the collapsing Stock Market or the Battlefield. We were gathering the fruits that ivied walls of college and university had planted and nurtured. Now in this time of our lives we were becoming the movers and shakers, homemakers, child-rearers. The weight of ever increasing responsibility to home and work and community called us to lean heavily on God, seek earnestly his guidance, acknowledge our weakness - allow ourselves to find strength, direction and a community of faith.

Chapter 7
THE HARD THINGS WELL

O NE CAN NEITHER BE TOO YOUNG OR TOO OLD TO IMPRINT LIFE WITH THE PRAYER: "GOD, HELP ME DO THE HARD THINGS WELL!" How often and in many circumstances it will be needed. The prayer "to do the hard things well" becomes a prayer not in the sense of passing an examination, or achieving the completion of a hard task, or the winning of a race. Rather in such instances as:

1) Taking leave of loved ones and friends
2) Forgiving and asking forgiveness
3) Turning the other cheek
4) Giving a soft answer to turn away wrath
5) Confronting prejudice and discrimination

Numerous stories come to mind, but this Junior High Camp story must be told. It contains the often wished-for but not realized effects of an act performed or an action carried out. Each Camp would receive funds - World Friendship moneys - to bring a student from another land, to broaden horizons and bring enrichment. This year the fund sponsored two Black students. Barbara and Jean were chosen, with their parents' consent, to live, and laugh, and play and pray with us.

As campers were moving into my cabin CRISIS AROSE! A bag was left in a family car. A call was made. Parents would return, not only to bring the bag, but to demand their daughters not live in the same cabin with our guests - else they would take their daughters home!! Camp Director, Mrs. English and I, who were responsible, were stunned and heart-sick. Tears, prayers, assurance, and commitment to Barbara and Jean, brought some calm and readiness for the evening ahead. After supper the pending confrontation came. Parents, director, counselor sat in faculty lodge, first praying together, placing all in God's hands, seeking His leading. The solution: our guests would join another cabin group who really wanted to make new friends. At the end of the week Barbara led Morning Watch with her prayer: *"Thank you, God, for all these wonderful friends and for this great week. AMEN."*

Come with me down the years. Conference youth leaders are to be installed. Alice was elected to chair of Christian Community. She called me aside: *Remember when I was a Junior Hi Camper? I graduated last week from high school. I was chosen to give the Valedictory Address. Going over it with my class teacher, she exclaimed: "You must tone down your words. People will never accept that we must change our attitudes toward other races!" I want you to know I gave my address! Now I am ready to be installed as officer for Christian Community, and serve God and youth to make a better world!*

This story is just a beginning of so many times through the years when forgiving, turning the other cheek, giving a soft answer proved to make all the difference - opening doorways, removing roadblocks - *"Help me do the hard things well!"*

THE SECRET

I met Christ in the morning when my day was at its best,
His presence came like sunrise, like a glory filled my breast
All day long His Presence lingered, all day long He stayed with me
And we sailed in perfect calmness o'er a very troubled sea.

Other ships were blown and battered; other ships were sore
distressed;
But the winds that seemed to drive them brought to me a
peace and rest.

Then I thought of other mornings, with a keen remorse of mind,
When I too had loosed the moorings with the Presence left behind.
Now I think I know the secret, learned from many a troubled way:
You must meet Him in the morning if you want Him through the day!

—Ralph S. Cushman

31

God, this is the first Sunday in Lent!
This is the time of preparation for deeper understanding
of the passion and death of Jesus Christ.
How can one prepare for it when one had little
experience with standing against evil?
What do I know of crucifixion?
How sensitive have I been to the personal hurt or
injury of another, now really?
I have rather stood by to admire and be sensitive
to the nobility of the spirit crushed, which
rose humbly again and in the experience
found a glow or light which makes them
lovable, gentle, kind.
God,
Let me hate the subtleties of INJUSTICE,
PREJUDICE, JEALOUSY, MALICE,
Help me to detect them!

Chapter 8
IN AWE OF PASSIONATE PLEAS

Whenever the pastor, or members of the congregation, kneel at the altar to pray God enters visibly with forgiveness, grace, healing, Presence.

From earliest years worship, and God and Love summon awe, reverence, curiousity...We want to know what happens in other congregations - the background from which their experiences are born.

We may find that worship is enhanced when we participate fully, led by those who would act out in movement, their adoration and praise. Black and Latino expressions in worship are uniquely theirs, and yes, even the Deaf community. Praying the Lord's Prayer in American Sign Language, necessitates the use of hands and head and heart - total concentration on words Jesus gave to his disciples.

In our White Anglo Saxon Protestant tradition, the outpouring of ourselves - BODY, MIND, and SPIRIT, was prohibited. The Augustinian tradition taught depravity of man - the human condition in need of the Church's redemption, overlooked the nature of God - Creator who declared all He made to be GOOD. God, who is LOVE, available to ALL HIS CHILDREN, EVER SEEKING THEM, AS THEY COME TO SEEK AND FIND HIM!

Until there comes into individual life unfathomable hurt, disaster, crucifixion - deep wounds of body, mind or spirit, does one find depths of new and grand proportion. When one suffers with a Beloved, watches a child die, the Holocaust happen, meets a survivor of Hiroshima, or a Killing Field in Cambodia, we may remember the words of John Donne: "Do not ask for whom the bell tolls, it tolls for thee."

It does not matter the manner one "draws near to the heart of God", only that it is precious and effective, and brings release, and hope, and Shalom.

HEAR MY PRAYER

Hear my prayer, O Lord, incline Thine ear!
Thyself from my petition do not hide;
Take heed to me!
Hear how in prayer I mourn to Thee!
Without Thee all is dark, I have no guide.

> *The enemy shouteth*
> *The godless come fast!*
> *Iniquity, hatred, upon me they cast!*
> *The wicked oppress me,*
> *Ah, where shall I fly?*
> *Perplexed and bewildered,*
> *O God, hear my cry!*

>> *My heart is sorely pained within my breast,*
>> *My soul with deadly terror is oppressed,*
>> *Trembling and fearfulness upon me fall,*
>> *With horror overwhelmed, Lord, hear my call!*

O for the wings of a dove!
Far, far away would I rove!
In the wilderness build me a nest
And remain there forever at rest.

Words by W. Bartholomew are set to music by Felix Mendelssohn and often sung by the Gregg Smith Singers.

APRIL 21, 1959

I plucked the fragile violet
And held it long within my hand
And pondered
> *This is Thy creation - this flower on stem*
> *steam on root hidden deep within the warm brown sod.*
> *This is of thee - a living thing -*
> *Its mystic loveliness filled my being*
> *with such compulsion that I gathered it*
> *from its source and took it for myself.*
> *I saw a part of Thee,*
> *and took it with all rapture unto me.*
> *I can't forget that fleeting note of sadness*
> *as soon with me the fragile violet faded.*

I wonder, God, have you made all living things
> *All beauty and growing things,*
> *all men, women and children*
> *of generations past and generations to come -*
for me to love, and tend, and nurture, but never again to pluck
from its source deep within the sod,
deep within
the heart of God?

CLEAR CHANNELS

APRIL 29, 1959

I'm beginning to understand, God, the significance of
*   clear channels.*
I would keep channels between me and thee open.
Now I see that the way to do this is to tear out
*   roots and twigs that block the channel*
*   between myself and my fellow men.*
These roots and twigs can be labeled -
*   - FEAR, fear of what others may think*
*   - DESIRE, desire to have the last word*
*   - UNWILLINGNESS, unwillingness to listen*
*   - UNDERSTANDING, understand what others*
*   really want.*

I WOULD BE A HUMBLE INSTRUMENT IN THY HANDS
I WOULD KNOW WHEN TO LISTEN - WHEN TO RESPOND

Evening comes, The day closes.
I listen, to the voice within,
Feel sunlight of the day warm from Thee.
Hush, to rest.
Another day is about to be born!

Chapter 9
DEEPER ROOTS

S eat belts fastened! The No Smoking signal on! We were preparing to land. Darkness out the window, became dotted with flickering lights - like a million candles. A new chapter begins in South Florida, Dade County, Miami! A tropical wonderland -- royal poincianas, slender palm trees, Indian Village, Water Ways and banyon trees.

Every new experience is awesome at best, but it would be the banyon tree that held a special message for me. Curious trees, with ever new roots put down into the soil, anchoring the spreading foilage, forming a canopy, shedding rain, a haven for birds. No hurricane could topple them!

God, you do appear in unexpected ways and places
to allay trepidation, inspire courage to meet new challenges.
May my roots sink deeper into your love and care
as new branches grow and foliage expands
to form a perfect image of your will for your children!

These "branches" would touch White Temple teens at a retreat in the Blue Waters Hotel, Miami Beach! Ocean waves rising high outside would not deter the fun, fellowship and great plans being made for a year of challenge, inspiration, service and worship. The simulated Garden of Gethsemane in Biscayne Park. In a hidden corner tall, angular Dave would kneel at the big rock in Biscayne Park, while MYF led a Holy Week worship experience. Missions. We would go to Havana, meet Ornan Iglesis, our missionary, who would take us through the countryside to see where a well-baby clinic was desperately needed. We would stay at the Theological Seminary in Matanzas, meet students, practice our Spanish.

Serving in this community, at the time not more than sixty years old, called for coping with forces promulgating against the Church, confronting segregation, learning from our Black brothers and sisters, finding Latino friends, serving Jamaicans, migrants and tourists! Over a quarter of a century White Temple's pastor Glenn James was a strong voice of conscience for the city of Miami. White Temple (Methodist Episcopal) and Trinity (Methodist Church South) just two blocks apart eventually united to become First United Methodist Church of Miami on Biscayne Boulevard, a timeless and strong Christian witness in that unusual city.

That group who met in the Blue Waters Motel long ago, September, 1953, are ALIVE TODAY! The bond of Christian Love has sustained them across the years. They have expanded, moved across the world, yet come together through letters and yearly reunions.

THEY TOO, LIKE THE BANYON TREE, PUT DOWN ROOTS INTO THE SOIL OF GOD. LINKED ARMS TO REACH EVER-WIDENING HORIZONS TO THE WORLD, THE GLOBAL COMMUNITY, THE KINGDOM OF GOD.

A few members of the original group should be named: *Joy Norton McGary, Opal and Larry Winebrenner, Ruth and Paul Fink, David Steel, Beverly, Jeanette. We mourn the loss of Ruth and Jean and others as age comes to all of us.* I am proud to be on the Templer's Roll!

AUGUST 1, 1959

> *God, you are STRENGTH like the rocky hills*
> *May I feel thy strength surging within me.*
> *God, you are PATIENCE. You work through*
> *long centuries with your children,*

that they may look into your face and not fear.
God, you are LIFE, the very surging blood
within our veins.
God, you are LOVE, unbounded love
the cord that binds
all mankind together!

SEPTEMBER 15, 1959 (Upon moving to a new neighborhood)

It's an awesome step, a heavy step
To become a part of a new community,
But a step firmly planted, there to live.
How does one become a part
     of the fabric of a neighborhood?
Does God work through the milieu
of human beings, new to each other?
I question!
     Alone with doubts.
   But tenaciously hold!

And then a knock at the door!

Laughing, smiling, eager eyes!
   "We're having a carnival,
We need some old clothes."
And another visit to play and sing.
Brief illness turned them aside.
Then came a knock. "My mother sent
   this home-made cake. She hopes you are better."

How does one become a part of a city, a community,
   a new neighborhood? LET GO. LET GOD!

JUNE 4, 1959 — CARAVAN TRAINING TIME

O God,
Forty folk this morning prepare for summer-time service to Thee
and Thy Church
Wilt thou be so very present, that all clear channels
will conduct thy spirit
from soul to soul, 'til the fabric
of all lives touched
be strengthened for
greater service to thy Kingdom!

JULY 5, 1959 (Caravan Training concludes, Hendricks College, Conway, Arkansas)

....That these might know thee, as God and Father
That they might be on the road, discovering the reality of
- love of God first
- then love of men.
That the CARAVAN PROGRAM might make realistic
the nature of the Christian fellowship
That a climate of love might prevail
leader with leader
youth with youth
to the end that God becomes reality.

Creative Years-
Retooling

Vacations are essential, as are Sundays, and Retreats!
When the Master Teacher needs go apart for a little while
- to refresh, take stock, be filled anew, correct direction, and
in essence, "empty himself again" then find clear again the
direction to go - so should we, for the same reasons!

Chapter 10
STURDY STEMS - NEW INSIGHTS

I loved New York, even before its logo came into existence. Early in my sojourn near Syracuse, I came across a gold mine: Chapel House, on the campus of Colgate University, Hamilton, New York. Chapel House is a gift built from the dream of a friend who had a friend who was a missionary in Burma. Feeling she had done little in comparison, Chapel House is now a memorial to a Baptist laywoman. A library, music room, refectory, and six guest rooms serve as a retreat spot. The Chapel is central and for all worshippers. Yellow stained glass allows the sun to always shine. A simple thin cross stretching from ceiling to floor is a permanent symbol. The outer rim of the chapel contains booths, for those who would practice worship of God in their own secret place.

Notes in my Journal attest to spirit-growth. In the midst of riches from the major religions of the world, one has the opportunity to read in the Koran, touch the hem of Zen, see the Smiling Buddha, hear the Temple Gong calling us to meals, listen to a Cantor at Sabot Service. In the music room one can hear Monks of the Weston Priory, John Coltrain's "Love Supreme," music from the world of Islam.

JOURNAL NOTES

ON ZEN MEDITATION

A young scholar went to a Master to learn. Tea was being served. The cup filled, the Master called for more, more, until the young scholar said, "But it is already full, Master." The Master then quietly said: "When one wants to learn anything from others, he must first empty himself; otherwise, there is no room for the new teachings to enter."

FROM GOETHE

"...then only are we thinking when the subject on which we are thinking cannot be thought out."

"SOULS ON FIRE"

"My father, an enlightened spirit, believed in man.
My grandfather, a fervent Hasid, believed in God.
The one taught me to speak, the other to sing.
Both loved stories,
And when I tell mine, I hear their voices
Whispering from beyond the silenced storm.
They are what links the survivor to their memory."

—Elie Wiesel

"MEMOIRS" 1975

In a preface to the book "CAT ON A HOT TIN ROOF" he talks of his goal in writing, namely: to somehow capture the constantly evanescent quality of existence. "I write so often of people with no magnitude, at least on the surface. I write of little people. But, are there little people? I sometimes think there are only little conceptions of people. Whatever is living and feeling with intensity is not little, and examined in depth, it would seem to me that most little people are living with that intensity that I can use as a writer.

—Tennessee Williams

43

ON WHOLENESS

Have you wondered why so many persons (of all ages) experience depression, seek suicide, or succumb to the drug culture? I have. Mary Caroline Richards in her book CENTERING (Wesleyan University Press, Middletown, CT) sheds light for me.

"The so called science and so called religion of our day, in the civilization of the West, tend to conduct a cold-war of their own.

"They tend to co-exist and divide the worlds between them. The split obstructs the poetic consciousness. Warring impulses beset the personality. Divisions and mutual suspicions grow as between one's inner sense of one's self and the social role one feels one is expected to play; between one's true feelings and social taboos, between the life that is offered and the life one wants. The inner soul withdraws, goes underground, splits off from the part that keeps walking around. Vitality ebbs. Psychic disturbance is acute. Suicide may be attempted.

"When a victim is fortunate enough to be healed he is as it were, reborn. For what were separated have undergone a metamorphosis into a new unity which allows the person to live as the person he is in society as it is.

"He finds a way to be a poet and a citizen. He finds a way to be himself and also the son of his parents. He finds a way to connect what lies within himself and what lies without. Having become, to some degree whole himself, he shows a tenderness toward others which is far different from the fear and contempt which characterized him formerly. At the same time having experienced the consequences of his own sick sensitivity, he has a capacity to be resolute with the sensitivity of others."

EVEN AS A POTTER CENTERS THE CLAY ON HIS WHEEL, SO WE WOULD BE CENTERED IN THEE, O GOD.

ON EDUCATION

I copied the following thoughts into my Journal while I was at Chapel House. Unfortunately, I neglected to note the author and title of the book.

"I am a teacher therefore I am interested in search and growth, schools and methods. Or does it work the other way around? I am interested in questions of meaning and technique. Since teaching and learning cannot be avoided, what can we contribute to the natural process? **What kind of environment and inner activity take us toward rebirth rather than toward perpetuation?**"

A teacher listens to what a child is telling him through his body, behavior, fantasies and play and speech. He does not try to apply a form conceived in advance, although patterns of growth have much in common and one can build up a knowledge of man and child which serves as a flexible method. This kind of reasoning occurs in every craft, in relation to a child's temperament, not against it...helps a child toward his individuality. **This is what no teacher must sin against. He helps a child be free of the ignorance and fear and clumsiness and compulsive treachery which may oppress his being. It is a terrible thing when a teacher does not care what a child does. It is fake and unfaithful. He seeks to understand what the child hungers for in the life of his imagination, his mind, his senses, his emotions, his will...he does not take things at face value but sees elements in relation to a life time process of deep structure.**

Since the very soul of the child's surroundings comes with life in his body, the early years are drastic in relation to later health. They help shape the body's hardness or softness, tension or ease. Later these tendencies are transformed into sickness or health. The child of an angry parent may develop disorder. The child of an indifferent parent may develop respiratory diseases.

ON THREE FREEDOMS

FREE PERCEPTION leaves the senses freely to follow the movement of form as it occurs, unobstructed by habit, anxiety, or unconcern.

FREE INITIATIVE, ability to create a future uncoerced by the past, is based upon self-knowledge and is a fruit of maturity.

FREE PARTICIPATION is the ability to unite with others, to collaborate, to identify with whatever human materials are at hand and is basically artistic in nature. It means a sense of spontaneity.

To live as artists in the moods and materials of life!
To use our plasticity,
yet to seek the truth of being and inner form that belong to us in-
dividually or as a living clay vessel to discover and take our form
in freedom and obedience.
Not to sell ourselves short as less interesting,
less beautiful and stirring and mysterious than the
  things we make.
And to realize that we do not win our depths and our inner
  form and our texture and our truth
of being without the fire. Ordeal by fire —
There is no substitute for transformation of the body.
I want students to be spontaneous, and energetic;
and at the same time sensitive, aware, composed.
I want them to be on fire;
at the same time I want the flames to be healing.
I want the flame of life out of which the phoenix is born —
Fire in the stone, which purifies, transforms, enkindles!

Life Extremes

I said to the Man at the Gate of the Year:
"Give me a light that I may tread out into the unknown."
He said:
"Go, place your hand in the hand of God;
It is safer than a light
And better than a known Way."

Chapter 11
HANDLING CONFLICT - LET GO, LET GOD

There are many times in the course of an adult life when frustration, doubt, anger, disbelief, cloud our hours, moments, days. Matthew Fox, in his book *Original Blessing*, would classify these under the heading of VIA NEGATIVA - state of pain, disease, nothingness. This personal prayer comes out of one of these times; the exact situation of no import, but the prayer, cry, no less real.

Oh, God,

Help me see my way through, know what I do in handling conflict, and know where it is health or non-health. I can choose
    to bow to...acquiesce
    to patronize
    to run away - escape
I'm prone to do the latter!

God, if I really know you and acknowledge you to be Reality,
then I know that all cannot be beauty and light,
that all cannot be perfection
that the world is so made that each of us in it
fails, and falls, and rises again.
We realize our inadequacy and our deep need of Thee,
    and thy Love and Grace, and in turn,
    accept fully and surely strength from thy hand and
know I cannot drift beyond thy love and care.

May I, in turn, accept those about me, in love,
Though I may not like him, he is after all A PERSON
FOR WHOM CHRIST DIED. WE ARE BROTHERS
AND SISTERS.

If I can, as we work on together,
feel and sense the faith and trust others have in me,
and confidence that I can do my task,
then I shall again experience the meaning of thy sustaining power
I would like especially, God, that this relationship be sustained,
and that I not run away from a task that is hard,
but give Thee increasing thanksgiving, that
Thou dost give tasks that are hard to do.

In this moment, God, allow this soul struggle to manifest
itself in ways that permit thy spirit and free-flowing love
to move out in ever widening circles.
It matters not where I am and with whom I work, but that
each daily task be done toward a common yet Universal good!

Ye shall know the truth, and the truth shall make thee free!

Kirkegaard speaks of "being the truth in all relationships
and in such manner that we are the manifestation of the
laws of the universe."

SUNDAY, APRIL 30, 1961

I have a little island deep inside
It isn't very long. It isn't very wide.
I really did not know that it existed
Until, one morning in a dream persisted
The image of a child.

An orphaned child came to abide
His future hope in me confide
It was pure coincidence
But it was meek and mild.

It is my way to very busy be
Involved, me thought, throughout eternity
DOING and GOING
THINKING and PLANNING
Always, of energy, most demanding
Obedience to a multitude.

But my discovery of both child and isle
Arrested for a little while
My busy search for meaning in time and space
And flowed in like a cooling stream of grace
A new dimension.

Chapter 12
LONESOME VALLEY

How blest we are! From earliest years music teachers introduced us to "Swing Low, Sweet Chariot." In Summer Camp we sang "We are Climbing Jacob's Ladder." There are times when Negro Spirituals speak to our very soul. I don't remember when the spiritual "Jesus Walked that Lonesome Valley," began "singing me," the verse becoming more and more audible taking on personal meaning:

> *You must walk that Lonesome Valley*
> *You've got to walk it by yourself.*
> *Oh, nobody else can walk it for you.*
> *You've got to walk it by yourself.*

This is stark reality. It comes to everyone. We must face our own mortality. It happens in many ways, at unexpected times. That reality experienced, realized, brings with it a freedom. Freedom from fear, freedom to grasp each day, to live with joy and hope and sensitivity to all of God's creation, and a readiness to connect with another traveler through the fields.

A day in the hospital clinched my awareness of my mortality. Family members helped me face this reality, in uniquely different ways:

My mother, succumbing to leukemia in her 63rd year, quietly gave last messages, testimony to her faith. To me: "He's coming for me now. It is all right." To her husband, my father: "Take good care of yourself."

My father whose last message on a wee bit of paper in his writing portfolio: "To live in the heart and mind of others is not to die."

Aunt Edna, a career nurse, strong of faith, who believed "that no one should die along" is remembered by many - even in the nursing home - because she would "be there" when family could not, through a final hour. How aware she was of her personal mortality, yet finding strength in continuing to give of herself to others. A faithful letter-writer who kept a large family in touch with each other can never be replaced!

Aunt Alice, a retired art teacher/principal, lived alone in the little house on Mulberry St. after Grandmother died. Age can be stressful and bring loneliness. It was for her. Dad lived not far away. I was not there when she died, but I find in my Journal the following prayers:

APRIL 1, 1959 (upon learning of Auntie's illness)

One alone who breathes a prayer
Who reaches out to feel thy hand
Least though she be, can rest assured
Thou art fairly by her side
    Look, Thou, this day upon all souls
    Who, burdened with life's loneliness
    Reach the close of active day
    And slip along the edge of years.
        Her dream of life ebbs now away
        Her days of service cease to be
        Oh God, a bit of joy, of freedom
        A glimpse of Thee, this be my plea!...

AUGUST 3, 1959

How I've tried my best to play God -
To see through human life and existence
With my own feeble and narrow horizon,
When all along the world had been in Thy hands.
The beautiful spirit of Auntie, that comes
through - that expresses her very soul
in her latter days.
Oh, God, thy mysteries of life overwhelm me.
Thy purpose and thy plan for thy children
is so vastly wonderful. It is beyond all
human comprehension.
Into thy sure hands I commend her spirit and
mine this night.
Let me continue to love, to give love,
to souls starved for love through all of life.

SEPTEMBER 29, 1959

Auntie went to her heavenly home today.
O God,
May there be no more despair,
no more loneliness, no more feeling sorry,
But may there be much rejoicing, hours of gladness,
and a feeling of being at peace.
I'm grateful for the family into which I was
privileged to be born. Father, let me express
that gratitude in love and understanding.

OCTOBER 11, 1959

Blessed are they that mourn
for they shall be comforted.....

There is conflict of thought this night, my Father,
It relates to a concept of Eternal Life.
I've felt that it was dependent upon good works more than faith.
Where does one meet His Maker?
Is God, who constantly seeks his children,
seeking each alike?
What about the lonely folk?

God, we are bound up in the bundles of life
from which we cannot escape, nor do we chose to.
We are grateful for those who have given us the gift of life.
May I realize anew the cause for which I was born.

Chapter 13
RISE UP, BRETHREN!

I hear and read about injustice - man's inhumanity to man. I stand by. What can I do? I am only one person. I feel sad inside when fear binds me. Why do I not speak out? Sometimes timidly, cautiously I find a way. Write letters, pray. Pray for someone TO BE THERE, GO FOR ME. Like Atticus Finch in Harper Lee's novel TO KILL A MOCKINGBIRD. In my Journals I find I am best at writing out my consternation. Today I would send a letter to the Editor of the local paper, attend a community meeting to find ways to combat racism, or drugs, or join a Prayer Chain.

JOURNAL APRIL 15, 1986

U.S. RETALIATES - DROPS BOMBS ON LIBYA. Phil Donahue gathers reactions. California Congressman said: "An eye for an eye, and a tooth for a tooth only leave a lot of the world sightless and toothless." Nothing gained. Can it be U.S. already victim of its POWER - no longer has safe access to Europe & Mediterranean travel?

O God, it was the rag-tag band of disciples - a tiny minority, who - empowered by thy Spirit dared to speak out in a world numbed by POWER. I affirm the gift that is mine to be a political being, yet find it so easy to stay on the sidelines and say:
"We elected them! Let them do it."
How easy to ask: "Lord, is it I?"
Or with Peter respond: "I do not know Him!"

AT THE TIME OF CENTRAL AMERICAN ATROCITIES:

We pray that the numbness and dullness may disappear out of the hearts of all who sit in seats of power; who hold in their hands the precious one vote that will recognize rights of people to their personal power, to override the cold, inhuman machine called government, business, armaments. God, these our representatives are human beings. Imbue them with a spirit of courage, vision, compassion for humankind, a sensitive ear to those they represent, and an awareness of thy guiding hand in their midst. But more, O God, strengthen that band of persons who tirelessly pursue the cause of Thy Son, Jesus Christ. Finally accept our humility, forgive our weakness and pour into our lives strength and direction for the living of these days. AMEN.

God,

It was a long time ago
you showed us the only way
your Love, and Life and Truth
might continue to be followed
in your world.

It was a way of crucifixion
of YOUR ONLY BEGOTTEN SON.

History has shown us that you have
many sons who have been
slain and the pattern
goes on, and on, and on...

Are we so unheeding and blind,
God, that we need so many
IN OUR DAY?

Grace Experienced

When life is shot through with the wonder and beauty and glory of God, when the God who is Love stoops down to touch, lift, rise within us, then does life become organized, directed, inspired. We know ourselves to be of recognizable and inestimable worth.

Chapter 14
BY WORKS, BY GRACE, BY GOD

The constant struggle oft seems ridiculous - the struggle to understand why GRACE is more important than WORKS. Jesus dealt with this and the sensitive soul continues to confront the dilemma.

For me it began in college. Sunday School Teacher, Mrs. Webster, constantly tried to get us to understand GRACE. Those days were times of gleaning, exploring, going through NEW DOORWAYS. It seemed that DOING was essential. GRACE seemed so very inert. My world was expanding, and my real world was exploding daily with World War II bombings, fellow students being called into the Draft, sent overseas, never to return! I needed to be ON THE FRONT LINES, too!

For me GRACE would be a concept, an experience to GROW INTO. Somewhere "through my fields" I met up with theologian Paul Tillich. The message in his book *THE COURAGE TO BE* surfaced again and again. DOING for me had not really meant what I sensed many times, for many people, in many churches, namely: EARNING GOD'S FAVOR through good deeds, through BEING GOOD. Gradually TO BE, first meant to me TO BE THERE for others, and then after touching many lives in times of extremities, I found myself in the presence of GIANTS (persons whose lives held much GREATNESS, but who were diminishing/diminished. I found myself saying again and again in the presence of such a one: "DOING may be over, but you are BEING to so many around you." The answer to the question: WHY AM I HERE? God intends that your "Light still shine!" It takes "COURAGE TO BE" in the midst of life's little or large challenges!

Bless JOHN WESLEY! And those preachers who keep talking about PREVENIENT GRACE! God indeed loved us even before we were a gleam in our parents' eyes! He LOVED us. He LOVES us because of ourselves, in spite of ourselves and our shortcomings, and not for what we do or will do, become or not become. For LOVE is God WITHIN! We need only to claim it.

Defining GRACE, for me has, for some reason, been difficult. BUT my JOURNAL WRITINGS confirm for me that GRACE, EXPERIENCED, is God's work over and over again, when paths are steep and rocky, level and grassy, unclear or well-marked!

MORE JOURNAL GLEANINGS!

JULY 15, 1984

> God,
>> You are so amazingly wonderful
>> You birthed and nurtured
>> You taught and demonstrated
>> Through the life of Jesus Christ
>>> and even in his dying
>> The richness and fullness of life
>>> eternal and everlasting
>>> Too numerous to name are your gifts. I'll try:
>>> Agility, mobility, facility, creativity, procreativity
>>>> strength, endurance, activity
>>>> rest, breathing, hearing, seeing,
>>> smelling, tasting, eating, drinking
>>>> talking, thinking, feeling.

Learning, memorizing, recalling, remembering
Deducing, synthesizing, refining, refreshing,
Theorizing, reconnoitering, imagining, realizing, recording

Loving, transcending, abiding, coping
Rejoicing, weeping, caring, hoping
Protecting, enabling, forgiving, understanding
Adoring, praying, enriching
YOU ARE AN AWESOME GOD!

JUNE 1985 - FATHER/MOTHER GOD

Very special - Significant - that moment
when it surfaced and enfolded me
in a blanket of warmth and wonder,
the Image of God as Mother!
It happened as I browsed thru books in a Provident bookstore.
Then melted away the struggle
that had been mine - a feeling, a lack
of a mother-love.
My Godhead Image grew.
Bringing Peace, and Wonder and Praise.

HE IS AND HE IS NOT -
MAMA, DADDY, FRIEND, LOVER,
UNTIL TWO BECOME ONE,
AND WHEN THRU DEATH THERE IS ONLY ONE AGAIN,
'TIS THEN I FIND SO VERY REALLY THAT
GOD IS LOVE!

JULY 1986 - THE LECTIONARY IN OUR LIVES

Selections from the Old and New Testaments and Letters to the early Churches, guide the sermonizers. Three diverse strains of thought and experience often cause the reader to skim, question, and move on wondering "how" and "why" any relevance might be found. THEN I DISCOVERED THE LECTIONARY *IN THE "NOW" OF MY LIFE!*

What is my lectionary? It is a human experience - in the life of another, transmitted to where I am, and its relevance to the "now" of another "in Christ"!

> *I tread humbly,*
> *I feel awe, wonder, trust,*
> *I know a soul-dimension, and a spirit-filled world*
> *So PRESENT NOW - yet, SPANNING timelessly -*
>   *AGES PAST,*
> *And AS FAR DOWN THE FUTURE*
> *As GOD ORDAINS TO BE!*

Chapter 15
THE BEST IS YET TO BE

How many times I ask of the poet: "What did you really mean when you wrote the words:

> "Grow old along with me
> The best is yet to be.
> The last of life is that for which the
> First was made...."

Did you really mean that? How can I know WHAT THE LAST OF LIFE REALLY IS? I'M NOT THERE YET!! There are times when I wonder: will I live to be 100? I hear people say: "I do not want to live that long." Then I take the hand of my very special nursing home resident, 103! And ask is she really just existing? I recall the days she walked through the hall - wig on head, cane in hand, proud - knowing all, yet not really known. I call her name as I lay my hand on hers. Her eyes lift up to mine: "How nice and warm you are." I fetch an afghan to put around her shoulders. I ask: of myself. "Who is she there for?" Could it be for me? I must go to see her today! Tomorrow may be too late. Can I really "be there" for her? Gentle conversation or none at all, not in a hurry, recalling if possible things I know of her earlier days. No matter time. This is "spirit-communion time."

If the FIRST OF LIFE is that important, what elements do those early years contain that affect one's later years?

The reality Jesus taught: "Where two or three are gathered in my name, there I am also." - is one element.

This reality is found in the bonds of marriage, continuing through life's verities and joys. Bonds with children and extended family, or commitment to responsible living under one roof, also reflect His teaching.

Wednesday evening Prayer Meetings! Passionate pleas on the part of the faithful few, are the keystone supporting the Body, the Church in any place. Small groups are essential.

A small group involved in *The Power and Light Company*, a study experience, are, ten years later, intimately involved in the life and works of their congregation. Realizing this, they begin a new cycle, that others may have that same experience that directs, reforms, renews all life and relationships.

Blessed will be that church where there comes together all who seem to be no longer relevant because of age or station, or monetary contribution. No one isolated. Alone!

The BEST IS YET TO BE?   Without question!

By John and Adrienne Carr

An experiential program based on Ephesians.

GARDEN

The garden, robed in spring-time mist at sunset hour
Bespoke of thee, until deep within,
The soul of me cried out in wonder,
kneeling before the radiance
of the flaming azalea bush
refreshed with perfume
so subtle that only the honeysuckle
can surpass.
My soul, still kneeling
touched the delicate petals of the pansy
and forget-me-not, the shooting star,
and candy-tuft.
The shrub and bleeding heart
stirred childhood memories
of Grandmother's garden!

Then came refreshing waves of gratitude
for that gift so precious, so real, so sacrificial
That GIFT OF LIFE and HERITAGE.

My soul, refreshed, rose from its knees,
and stretched far into the cool of eventide
as if to join with Him
WHO WALKS IN A GARDEN,
WHO PRAYS IN A GARDEN
WHO WAS THE SON
OF THE MASTER-GARDENER!

SEPTEMBER 1, 1984

I WANT TO GO BACK FOR A LITTLE WHILE
   Not to run away
   Nor regress
   Nor to pick up an unfinished chapter
      in my Book, My Life.

I want to go back for Auld Lang Syne
To visit those from former years
   who so loved life and living things
   creepy crawly green and growing and
   shared that joy with me.

To recall, reminisce,
   but best, to remember -
Breaking Bread at their table,
Sharing gifts from the good earth,
Nourishment for body, mind and spirit.

I want to go back to find
   the children I'd known
   Tall, self-possessed and beautiful -
   taking hold of life - wide-eyed,
   eager to discover new strengths and dexterity
   that spawns gold medal standing
   in sports like Kayaking.
   Move from home to college dorm,
Dimensions of growing independence -
   Ties of childhood lessening
   New ties waiting, new found love,
   dreams, hopes, and aspirations.

Surprise! I am not alone
in "going back." I smiled
when Amy - in that brief visit,
produced the very game they used to play
as children - one last look at sheltered,
happy childhood years.
What priceless moments they recall.
Truly one of the mysteries and joys
of human mind and heart.

New Creation

I am a part of it. You are a part of it. We live far beyond the magic date for retiring. We are relevant, we are keepers of the faith, we are the embodiment of our dream. The past does have a design worthy of the future. We must, now, begin to affect these days, continue telling THE STORY, that our grandchildren, heirs, may have a New Creation!

Chapter 16
THE CHURCH STILL TEACHING

Its origin, beginning or ending is elusive. These words come to mind:

> *"Something's lost!*
> *Go and find it!*
> *MIGHTY MAKER, IS IT THOU???"*

I look out across the land. Read in the morning paper of the children figuratively abandoned to drug-infested neighborhoods, shuttled between parents too busy, too broken, too depleted themselves to nurture and pray and teach children, bonding them early to the God that is within them. How will they learn without a teacher?

A child prays:

"Dear God: My mom and dad are divorced. For three years. Nobody's perfect. But why did you pick on us? I wish we were all with each other. Maybe you could have them get along on weekends. Please, Stephen."

The adage that affected the raising of children of my generation - Children should be seen and not heard - has slowly eroded into unbelievable neglect. The sacredness of each child in our midst brings with it a mandate to make children PRIORITY ONE today. Permeating Central Pennsylvania Annual Conference recently was the theme: "LOVE A CHILD...CHANGE THE WORLD." Children were set in our midst. At one point every member of that large body intentionally named a child for whom to pray regularly.

Another sign of HOPE for Children comes through a Parish Newsletter - used as a TEACHING INSTRUMENT. Excerpts are here. Simple enough for "children" of any age to comprehend and practice.

WHAT IS PRAYER?

Prayer is talking to God. Prayer is listening to and learning what God wants to say to you. God loves and cares for you. God wants to help you and others. God wants you to pray to him every day.

Read the recipe for prayer here. There are four different kinds of prayer:

A-doration — praising God and telling God how wonderful he is.

C-onfession — telling God we are sorry when we do something wrong.

T-hanks — telling God we appreciate our blessings (things God has given us).

S-aying what is needed — asking God for help.

from The Champlain Circuit Rider
July 1996

Chapter 17
CLOUD OF WITNESSES

S t. Paul over 19 centuries ago reminded in one of his letters that "WE ARE SURROUNDED BY SO GREAT A CLOUD OF WITNESS" that "WE TOO MUST PRESS ON TOWARD THE GOAL, THE HIGH CALLING WHICH IS IN CHRIST JESUS." I am grateful for his Letters to Timothy, reminding him of the faith of his GRANDMOTHER EUNICE AND HIS MOTHER LOIS.

How precious are those who launched us on our way; believed in us when we were not yet ready to believe in ourselves. The birthers and nurturers, the mentors and teachers, those with whom we were in work-fellowship, and those who in the midst of conflicts, DARED TO STAND SURE AND FIRM.

MY GRANDMOTHER, LAURA, who sat in her bay window on Sundays reading her Bible. She was the gardener who knew even the botanical names of every flower, and who lived to be 95 years old.

MY MOTHER AND FATHER, Ethel (O'Brien) and John Hess.

SISTER CYNTHIA KOHLER, childhood friend, who faithfully keeps me in her prayers, and I her, as she ages and lives with emphysema at Holy Family Convent.

DR. AND MRS. J. HOWARD AKE; I can't believe I faithfully followed his Sunday Evening study *PILGRIM'S PROGRESS*. (Was it because my date and I were together?). MRS. AKE came to me following my months in "Darkness" and invited me to "join the church," nudging me into many new experiences. I remember her report from the GENERAL CON-

FERENCE WHEN THREE BRANCHES OF METHODISM UNITED! What a lady!

REV. LESTER A. SCHAFF, college pastor, Mansfield, PA - an inspiration, a friend across the years, a believer in me. A poet at heart.

DR. AND MRS. EDWIN KEBOCH (MABEL), Executive Secretary Central Pennsylvania Conference Board of Education, on whose staff I served as Youth Director, and continued in work-fellowship across the years.

FREDDIE HENRY SCHISLER, Scarritt College Professor. Education of Children in the Church, to become a colleague in the Editorial Division and friend who, introduced me to Early American Glass.

DR. CHARLES LAYMAN, New Testament Professor, Scarritt College. Beloved is that person who bestows upon us the treasures of the New Testament. Did he really have a hand in my coming to the Methodist Editorial Division, when he was Editor of Adult Publications?(!)

BISHOP FELTON AND PHYLLIS MAY - my Bishop for 12 years!! My rare privilege to be named to Board of Diaconal Ministry as Registrar, by him, but so much more as he brought people of my Annual Conference to reconciliation, forgiveness, for acts of prejudice toward any of God's children. Love and affection and prayers go with them as they go to serve Washington Area of the United Methodist Church.

MRS. MARCUS RANDALL - HAZEL - who after her husband's death prayed for a friend. When I came to York, to find her in the same church, I became her answer to prayer! I indeed am blessed with A FRIEND of 15 years!

And unnumbered are those persons who form a network - a safety net - that keeps us from falling, adds sustenance, and support when needed, and allows us to live fully and completely in God's love!

EPILOGUE

LISTEN! HEAR! DARE! REJOICE! GIVE THANKS!

Remember singing the chorus: "WHEN HE CALLS ME I WILL ANSWER, I'LL BE SOMEWHERE LISTENING, FOR MY NAME," but surely not in the wee hours of the morning?

I have a tiny plaque on my desk that refuses to get lost:

I
GET
MY BEST
IDEAS
WHEN I
AM SLEEPING!

I do! And must arise at 5:00 a.m. to capture those good ideas and put them down on paper. Not long ago I was vindicated. Charles Shulz captured my sentiments when Charlie Brown was aroused from sleep to find THAT BEAGLE, SNOOPY at the end of the bed with typewriter clicking away, saying those very words: "I GET MY BEST IDEAS WHEN I AM SLEEPING!"

DARE!

Gerontologists tell us that as we age, we may lose some of our timidity, inhibitions. We DARE speak out! Witness to God's love in Jesus Christ. But aren't we called to DARE daily? After LISTENING, of course.

It was in the late 60's. Martin Luther King had not yet been slain. Detroit was burning. I had taken my Confirmation Class to that very area of the city the week before to learn the church's part in getting schools open for breakfast for hungry children; how the church was to respond to Jesus' command: "As ye did it unto one of the least of these you did it unto me."

Shortly after a letter came offering me a position in the Evanston YWCA. Dare I answer? YES! The YWCA goal: TO ELIMINATE RACISM in its Institution. They would train. I would BE A PART OF IT!

Of late as I listen in the wee hours of the morning, I'm prompted to set sights toward a new goal. Then keep listening for directions on how I shall arrive!

REJOICE!

Last year I returned from Christmas with special gifts. The giver would have no idea and would undoubtedly wonder that I was meddling! THESE GIFTS I HEARD!

One person found a friend who would need her. Another had laid aside old animosities, and the newly-wedded couple shed "magical silver dust" on all, imparting joy and goodwill!!! REJOICE! GIVE THANKS AND SING!

As I deal with the aches and pains of aging, I return to that delightful children's book, THE LITTLE ENGINE THAT COULD. Daily my words "I THINK I CAN!" begin in the interior me and I meet the day with new promise!

I remember again my "ever-so-long-ago" encounter with Abraham. Still teaching home economics, I attended a Leadership School. Emergency arose. I was called to substitute for the lesson on Abraham! "Your descendants shall be as many as the stars in the heavens."

As I walked home that night, I looked up at the starry sky as was my usual practice. I may not know Abraham, I thought, nor have I descendants, but I do know the "stars in the heavens"! They were set there AT THE BEGINNING, AND WOULD BE SURE TO THE END OF TIME!"

JULY 1984 - GARDEN LESSONS FROM MY BACK YARD

My snapdragons are an awesome lot!
Not alone electric in their varying hues
almost iridescent in the early evening
when they seem to capture and hold on
to the waning rays of brilliant sunlight.
And then when it seems their time is spent
and wind and rain and heat of day
untie each tiny face and lay it gently on the ground,
It is then the Gardener comes and with a snip, a pinch,
removes the stem of seed pods.
It is then, so long as summer lasts
they replenish the spot where they grow
with new and brighter shining faces, until the time
of autumn and winter frosts may come!
And so, the MASTER GARDENER
in my three-score years and ten,
doth, at the time I think my work,
my day is nearing end, STOOPS TO TOUCH
AND, LO, I BLOOM AGAIN!

ACKNOWLEDGMENTS

To those who read, corrected, critiqued, and gave their blessing:

JANIS SNELL
ANNA MILLER
DONALD M. TREESE

To photographer friend, for cover photo:

GLADYS WIDEMIRE

To cover designer and illustrator:

BRENT COULSON

For permission to use words to the song, "MY GOD AND I".

Other permissions forthcoming, with promise to correct in second printing any inaccuracies that have been noted.

Poems are in public domain or copyrighted by the author.

Back cover Scripture from NRS Version of the Bible. Selected verses Psalm 78. Copyright © 1989 Div. CEd.NCCC USA.

LITTLE BOOK
GO FAR AND WIDE
BLESS THOSE WHO READ
IN LOVE ABIDE!

THE CIRCLE OF LIFE
A VISUAL BIOGRAPHICAL SKETCH
OF AUTHOR OF
THROUGH THE FIELDS

A native of Williamsport,
living in retirement in York, Pennsylvania.

My Journey
"Through the Fields"

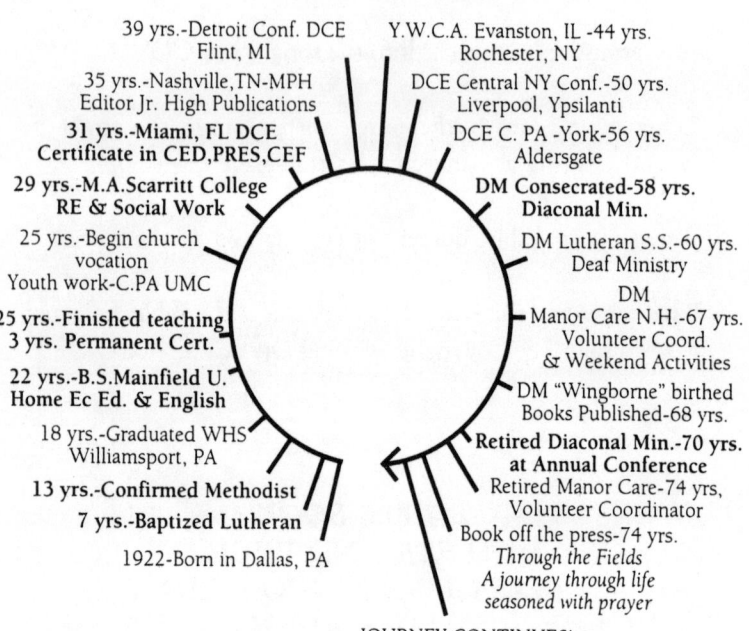

39 yrs.-Detroit Conf. DCE
Flint, MI

35 yrs.-Nashville,TN-MPH
Editor Jr. High Publications

**31 yrs.-Miami, FL DCE
Certificate in CED,PRES,CEF**

**29 yrs.-M.A.Scarritt College
RE & Social Work**

25 yrs.-Begin church
vocation
Youth work-C.PA UMC

**25 yrs.-Finished teaching
3 yrs. Permanent Cert.**

**22 yrs.-B.S.Mainfield U.
Home Ec Ed. & English**

18 yrs.-Graduated WHS
Williamsport, PA

13 yrs.-Confirmed Methodist

7 yrs.-Baptized Lutheran

1922-Born in Dallas, PA

Y.W.C.A. Evanston, IL -44 yrs.
Rochester, NY

DCE Central NY Conf.-50 yrs.
Liverpool, Ypsilanti

DCE C. PA -York-56 yrs.
Aldersgate

**DM Consecrated-58 yrs.
Diaconal Min.**

DM Lutheran S.S.-60 yrs.
Deaf Ministry

DM
Manor Care N.H.-67 yrs.
Volunteer Coord.
& Weekend Activities

DM "Wingborne" birthed
Books Published-68 yrs.

**Retired Diaconal Min.-70 yrs.
at Annual Conference**
Retired Manor Care-74 yrs,
Volunteer Coordinator
Book off the press-74 yrs.
*Through the Fields
A journey through life
seasoned with prayer*

JOURNEY CONTINUES!

SECOND DEDICATION

to
each in my
blessed community
community of the heart.

Since my "darkness" days when I hungrily committed to memory many words, - among them Margaret Sanger's....*MY ONLY PRAYER IS WHILE I LIVE "GOD MAKE ME WORTHY OF MY FRIENDS."* I have gathered a precious Community. It is best described below:

"Within the wider Fellowship emerges the special circle of a few on whom, for each of us, a particular nearness has fallen. These are our special gift and task. These we "carry" by inward, wordless prayer. Two people, three people, ten people may be in living touch with one another through Him who underlies their separate lives......We know that these souls are with us, lifting their lives and ours continuously to God and opening themselves, with us, in steady and humble obedience to Him. It is as if the boundaries of our self were enlarged, as if we were within them and as if they were within us. Their strength, given to them by God, becomes our strength, and our joy, given to us by God, becomes their joy. In confidence and love we live together in Him".

—Thomas Kelly, *A Testament of Devotion*

FOR THE READER:

<u>MY JOURNAL PAGES</u>

<u>NOTES ON MY VERY BEST / VERY WORST TIMES</u>

FOR THE READER:

WISDOM I WOULD LIKE TO
PASS ON TO OTHERS

FOR THE READER:

MY PERSONAL TIME LINE

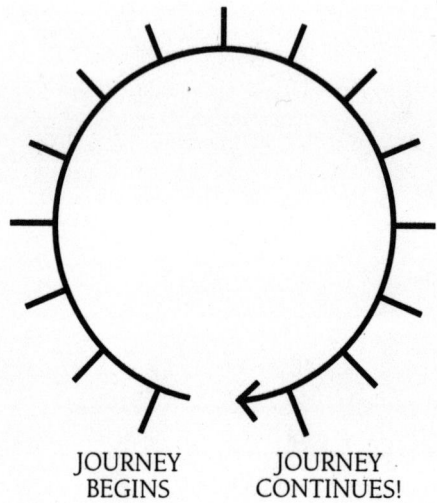

JOURNEY   JOURNEY
BEGINS   CONTINUES!